SandCastle™

Mini Animal Marvels

Miniature Reptiles

CHILDREN'S LIBRARY

A Division of ABDO

ABDO
Publishing Company

Alex Kuskowski   Consulting Editor, Diane Craig, M.A./Reading Specialist

visit us at www.abdopublishing.com

Published by ABDO Publishing Company, a division of ABDO, P.O. Box 398166, Minneapolis, Minnesota 55439. Copyright © 2014 by Abdo Consulting Group, Inc. International copyrights reserved in all countries. No part of this book may be reproduced in any form without written permission from the publisher. SandCastle™ is a trademark and logo of ABDO Publishing Company.

Printed in the United States of America, North Mankato, Minnesota
102013
012014

 PRINTED ON RECYCLED PAPER

Editor: Liz Salzmann
Content Developer: Alex Kuskowski
Cover and Interior Design and Production: Mighty Media, Inc.
Photo Credits: Shutterstock, Zach Welty, Nick Scobel

Library of Congress Cataloging-in-Publication Data

Kuskowski, Alex.
  Miniature reptiles / Alex Kuskowski.
    pages cm. -- (Mini animal marvels)
  ISBN 978-1-62403-069-7
1. Reptiles--Juvenile literature. 2. Reptiles--Size--Juvenile literature. I. Title.
  QL644.2.K87 2014
  597.9--dc23
                    2013022908

SandCastle™ Level: Transitional

SandCastle™ books are created by a team of professional educators, reading specialists, and content developers around five essential components—phonemic awareness, phonics, vocabulary, text comprehension, and fluency—to assist young readers as they develop reading skills and strategies and increase their general knowledge. All books are written, reviewed, and leveled for guided reading, early reading intervention, and Accelerated Reader® programs for use in shared, guided, and independent reading and writing activities to support a balanced approach to literacy instruction. The SandCastle™ series has four levels that correspond to early literacy development. The levels are provided to help teachers and parents select appropriate books for young readers.

Emerging Readers
(no flags)

Beginning Readers
(1 flag)

Transitional Readers
(2 flags)

. Fluent Readers
(3 flags)

Table of Contents

Miniature Reptiles

Miniature **reptiles** are very small reptiles. Lizards, alligators, and turtles are reptiles.

Pygmy Leaf Chameleon

Madagascar

The pygmy leaf chameleon is a lizard. It lives in the rain forest.

6 feet
(1.8 m)

It is 1¼ inches
(3.2 cm) long.

1¼ inches
(3.2 cm)

The pygmy leaf chameleon can change color. It looks like a leaf.

Green Anole

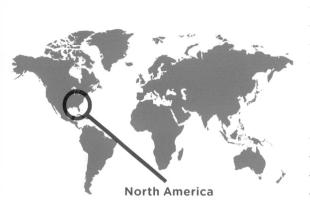

North America

The green anole is a lizard. It eats bugs and grass.

6 feet
(1.8 m)

It is 7 inches
(17.8 cm) long.

7 inches
(17.8 cm)

A green anole is usually green.
Sometimes it turns brown.

A **male** anole has a neck **flap**.
It can turn red. It can puff out.

Dwarf Caiman

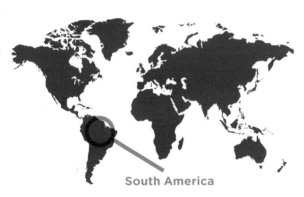

South America

The dwarf caiman looks like an alligator. But it is smaller.

It is 4½ feet (1.4 m) long.

6 feet (1.8 m)

4½ feet (1.4 m)

Dwarf caimans live near rivers. They hunt at night. They eat fish, frogs, and bugs.

Bog Turtle

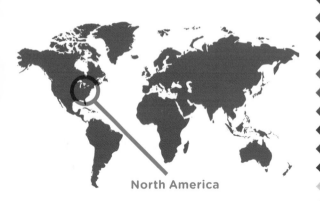

North America

The **bog** turtle is a very small turtle. It lives in North America.

6 feet
(1.8 m)

It is 4 inches
(10.2 cm) long.

4 inches
(10.2 cm)

Bog turtles are **cold-blooded**.
They warm up in the sun.

They sleep during the winter.
They lie in the mud.

Did You Know?

 Chameleons can move each eye separately.

 The green anole can grow a new tail.

 Dwarf caimans sleep in **burrows**.

 Turtles cannot leave their shells.

Reptile Quiz

1 The pygmy leaf chameleon can change color.

2 Green anoles sometimes turn brown.

3 A green anole's neck **flap** never puffs out.

4 Dwarf caimans live near oceans.

5 **Bog** turtles are **cold-blooded**.

Answers: 1. True 2. True 3. False 4. False 5. True

Glossary

bog – land that is wet and spongy.

burrow – a hole or tunnel dug in the ground by a small animal for use as shelter.

cold-blooded – having a body temperature that changes according to the temperature of the surroundings.

flap – a movable part that hangs from the side of something.

male – being of the sex that can father offspring. Fathers are male.

reptile – a cold-blooded animal that moves on its belly or on very short legs.